MAR 2 2 2016

GRAVES MEMORIAL LIBRARY
111 North Main Street
Sunderland, MA 01375

D0928106

Alligators
and Crocodiles

Diane Swanson

Gareth Stevens Publishing
A WORLD ALMANAC EDUCATION GROUP COMPANY

GRAVES MEMORIAL LIBRARY
SUNDERLAND, MA 01375

Please visit our web site at: www.garethstevens.com
For a free color catalog describing Gareth Stevens Publishing's list of high-quality books
and multimedia programs, call 1-800-542-2595 (USA) or 1-800-387-3178 (Canada).
Gareth Stevens Publishing's fax: (414) 332-3567.

The publishers acknowledge the support of the Canada Council for the Arts and the Cultural Services
Branch of the Government of British Columbia in making this publication possible.
The author thanks James Perran Ross, Crocodile Specialist Group, for his help.

Library of Congress Cataloging-in-Publication Data

Swanson, Diane, 1944-
    Alligators and crocodiles / by Diane Swanson.
       p. cm. — (Welcome to the world of animals)
    Includes index.
    Summary: Introduces the physical characteristics, behavior, and habitat of members of the
crocodilian family.
    ISBN 0-8368-4021-6 (lib. bdg.)
    1. Alligators—Juvenile literature. 2. Crocodiles—Juvenile literature. [1. Alligators.
2. Crocodiles.] I. Title.
    QL666.C925S97   2004
    597.98—dc22   2003059156

This edition first published in 2004 by
Gareth Stevens Publishing
A World Almanac Education Group Company
330 West Olive Street, Suite 100
Milwaukee, WI 53212 USA

MAR 2 '04

This U.S. edition copyright © 2004 by Gareth Stevens, Inc. Original edition copyright © 2002
by Diane Swanson. First published in 2002 by Whitecap Books, Vancouver. Additional end matter
© 2004 by Gareth Stevens, Inc.

Series editor: Betsy Rasmussen
Design: Melissa Valuch
Cover design: Steve Penner

Cover photograph: Stan Osolinski/Dembinsky Photo Assoc.
Photo credits: Wayne Lynch 4, 6, 14; Lynn M. Stone 8, 24; Tony Rath/ Naturalight Productions 10;
Rob and Ann Simpson 12; Dusty Perin/Dembinsky Photo Assoc. 16; Mark J. Thomas/Dembinsky Photo
Assoc. 18; Claudia Adams/Dembinsky Photo Assoc. 20; Jay Ireland and Georgienne Bradley 22, 30; Stan
Osolinski/Dembinsky Photo Assoc. 26, 28

All rights reserved. No part of this book may be reproduced, stored in a retrieval system, or transmitted
in any form or by any means, electronic, mechanical, photocopying, recording, or otherwise, without
the prior written permission of the copyright holder.

Printed in the United States of America

1 2 3 4 5 6 7 8 9 08 07 06 05 04

Contents

World of Difference

There is nothing puny about alligators and crocodiles. They are the largest reptiles alive. An American crocodile can stretch up to 15 feet (4.5 meters) in length and weigh up to 450 pounds (200 kilograms). Its jaws are huge. Its tail is powerful. And its skin is thick and tough, like armor.

Not all crocodilians (CROK-uh-DILL-yuns) — a group of animals that includes both alligators and crocodiles — grow as big as American crocodiles. Still, the common caiman, which is North America's smallest crocodilian, can grow 5 to 8 feet (1.5 to 2.5 m) long.

Sometimes mistaken for a small crocodile, the common caiman is an alligator.

A smiling reptile? No, but the curvy jawline of an American crocodile looks like a grin.

Of the more than twenty kinds of crocodilians in the world, four live in North America. They include two alligators (the American alligator and the common caiman) and two crocodiles (the American crocodile and the Morelet's crocodile).

You can tell alligators from crocodiles

by looking at their snouts. An alligator's snout is usually wide and rounded, but a crocodile's is more slender and pointed. Look at the teeth, too. When a crocodile's mouth is shut, you will spot a tooth close to the front of its bottom jaw on each side. Each of these side teeth pokes into grooves outside the top jaw. The same teeth on an alligator are hidden when its mouth is closed.

Like other reptiles, such as lizards, snakes, and turtles, crocodilians are scale-covered animals that produce little heat. They lie in the sunshine to warm up.

GREAT GATORS, INCREDIBLE CROCS

Here are some amazing things alligators and crocodiles can do.

- Alligators can pull their eyes into their skulls for protection.

- Crocodilians swallow rocks to help them digest food and float flat in water.

- The jaws of an American alligator are strong enough to crunch an aluminum canoe.

- A crocodile that died in a zoo in 1997 was 115 years old!

Where in the World

Wetlands and warm weather attract crocodilians. They have made homes in parts of Africa, Asia, Australia, and North, Central, and South America.

American alligators, common caimans, and Morelet's crocodiles live mostly in and around freshwater marshes, swamps, streams, lakes, and ponds. Sometimes they head into saltwater for a short time.

American crocodiles live in both freshwater and saltwater. Now and then, storms sweep them out to open sea. These crocodiles have special glands that help remove the extra salt their bodies take in.

The American alligator is right at home in a swamp.

A Morelet's crocodile slips into the stream to hunt.

When the weather is hot and dry, crocodilians may stay cool by digging burrows. They use their snouts, feet, and long strong tails to plow soft ground. American alligators may dig a tunnel that is longer than a car.

Alligators also burrow to escape cold weather. In the southern United States, they may have to survive freezing temperatures. They seldom eat when it is cold. Instead, they draw on energy stored in their bodies.

American alligators can even live through wintry blasts by floating in the water. If ice at the surface freezes around the alligators, they cannot move. But as long as their nostrils are poking above the surface, they are able to breathe. Then the alligators simply wait for a warm spell to set them free.

GATOR AID

American alligators help other animals. In dry seasons, wetland birds, fish, snakes, turtles, and insects depend on water stored in holes made where alligators wallow. In rainy seasons, alligator-made paths worn in soft ground help drain off extra water.

Alligators feed on animals that devour a lot of plants, often saving wetlands from overgrazing. By eating dead creatures, they act as cleanup teams, creating healthier homes for all.

World in Motion

All crocodilians get around just fine on land and in water, but they are best suited for swimming. With their tails gently swishing, they cruise near the surface with barely more than their eyes and nostrils poking out. When they chase something — or when something chases them — the animals whip their mighty tails in S-shaped curves and zoom ahead.

If crocodilians want to sink out of sight, it is easy. They simply flick their feet upward, spread out their toes, and down they go. They can close their nostrils and ears, which keeps the water out.

A long, strong tail powers a swimming crocodilian.

13

A common caiman can travel a long distance over land.

A crocodilian does not use its legs for swimming. It holds them close to its body. But the reptile can suddenly shoot out of the water and rush short distances on shore to snap at animals such as birds.

On land, a crocodilian often does the "high walk." It draws its legs under itself, lifting its body above the ground. The high walk prevents the animal's undersides from scraping against rocks.

You can probably outrun a crocodilian, but do not even think about trying! From a standing start, a crocodilian can reach full speed really fast.

If anything startles crocodilians, they usually head for water. They do the "belly crawl," sliding down over mud, or speed up to a "belly run." Pushing hard with their legs, they coast in curves and hit the water swimming.

TRAILING A CROC

Heading through a swamp, an American crocodile enters a snare. A cable of steel snaps tightly around its body. "Caught!" thinks the researcher as she slips a noose over the animal's snout. Then she tapes its jaws together.

Quickly, the researcher weighs, measures, and tags the crocodile. Then she removes the tape and frees the animal. For several days, she will follow it to see where it travels. She is learning that crocodiles need a lot of space.

World Full of Food

Crocodilians eat whatever crocodilians can. Big ones often grab big prey, such as turtles, herons, and deer. They also gobble up little frogs, crabs, and insects, just like smaller kinds of crocodilians and young ones do.

Some kinds chase after certain foods. Mud turtles, for instance, are a favorite food of the Morelet's crocodiles. But many crocodilians eat a lot of fish.

Resting in shallow water, a crocodilian waits to sense the movement of an approaching fish. Then, with a sudden snap of its jaws, it nabs the fish, pressing it against a streambed or lake floor to get

A turtle makes a good meal for a hungry alligator.

17

Gone fishing! A crocodilian gets ready to down its catch.

a solid grip. Next, the reptile pokes its head up above water and lets the fish drop down its throat. If the fish is especially large, the crocodilian might carry it ashore, holding or bashing it until it stops moving.

Surprise is what a crocodilian uses when it hunts. Blending in with floating plants, logs, and murky water, it swims slowly toward a wading bird, or it lunges for a bigger animal that is drinking from shore and drags it underwater.

A crocodilian has more than twice as many teeth as you have, but it cannot chew a thing. Small prey is gulped down whole. Large animals are torn into pieces. A crocodilian yanks and twists them until it rips off a chunk. In the process, the reptile might lose a few teeth, but that is no problem. Each tooth has a replacement, which soon moves into place.

TOSSING IT OUT

Owls do it. So do sharks. They cough up things they can't digest. It is a normal process and not a sign of sickness.

Healthy crocodiles bring up stuff they cannot use — such as hairballs — but they are not able to vomit forcefully. Instead, they jerk their heads as if they're sneezing. Then they snap their jaws and shake their snouts from side to side. All that action helps release the waste that rises up their throats.

19

World of Words

American alligators are especially chatty, but all crocodilians communicate with sound. They often make low-pitched sounds that travel well.

Alligators ready to mate may "cough" or "purr" to their mates. The soft noises carry only a short distance. But alligators can also bellow loudly, which seems to encourage other alligators to bellow, too.

If danger threatens, young crocodilians cry out, warning the others and calling adults for help. The grown animals — usually the parents — respond by threatening or attacking the enemy.

Close up, mating gators signal softly to each other.

Crocodile tears are a good thing. They help care for the eyes.

Making sounds is nothing new for young crocodilians. They start grunting when they are still inside their eggs — especially when they are ready to hatch. The grunts signal their parents to dig the eggs out of their deep nests.

Crocodilians use body language, such as head slapping, too. It is a way of announcing, "We're here!" They lift their heads just above water, then open and close their big jaws fast. The movement creates a loud POP and a splash. Some crocodilians follow up by blowing bubbles, thrashing their tails, or roaring.

Head slaps grab the attention of other crocodilians in the neighborhood. They may rush to the surface of the water to copy the head slap. The action helps bring many crocodilians together, especially during mating seasons.

CROCODILE TEARS

When people only pretend to feel sorry or sad, we say they are "crying crocodile tears." Alligators and crocodiles produce tears, but their "crying" has nothing to do with their feelings — either real or pretend.

Glands create moisture behind a crocodilian's extra eyelids — the see-through lids that protect its eyes under-water. Tears smooth the movement of the lids, help clean the eyes, and probably fight bacteria, too.

New World

Mother crocodilians lay tough, leathery eggs. Different kinds of crocodilians lay different numbers of eggs. American alligators produce about forty-five eggs, while common caimans lay only half that many.

First, the female crocodilians build nests. They choose spots that won't likely be flooded by heavy rains and rising waters. American crocodiles usually dig holes and cover them with plants. Sometimes, these crocodiles just pile up plants and mud — as Morelet's crocodiles, common caimans, and American alligators normally do.

Fresh out of their eggs, crocodilians greet a new world.

25

A young alligator hitches a ride on mom's long tail.

Like heaps of garden compost, crocodilian nests heat up as the plants inside them rot. That helps keep the eggs warm. For some crocodilians, the temperature of the eggs determines whether the hatchlings will be male or female. Warm eggs produce males; slightly cooler eggs produce females.

Crocodilian mothers often guard their nests for several weeks or months. They seldom leave — even to eat. The mother protects the eggs from animals such as lizards.

Most crocodilians break through their shells then wait for their mothers to dig them out of the nest. She may help any unhatched young by lightly cracking their eggs in her mouth.

Mother crocodilians — and some fathers — may scoop up a group of hatchlings in their mouths. Then they give the young ones a safe ride to a nearby pond or stream.

WHY, OH WHY?

Red-bellied turtles in Florida often lay eggs in American alligator nests. Alligators guarding their eggs from egg eaters, such as raccoons, just happen to protect turtle eggs, too. But these same alligators eat some of the newly hatched turtles!

Yet, more turtles may survive from eggs laid in alligator nests than from eggs laid elsewhere. If so, scientists wonder why. Does turtle survival depend on protection from egg eaters?

Small World

For safety reasons, young crocodilians stick together. During their first weeks or months, their mothers stay with them, too. An American alligator mom often looks after her young for two or more years.

Groups of newly hatched crocodilians usually stay close to their nests, with their parents or other adults nearby. The mature crocodilians sometimes make sounds that tell the young ones when food is near.

At times, the sounds turn to warnings of danger, such as when a hawk swoops low or a big fish swims close by. Adult crocodilians also defend their young by

The yellow bands on young American alligators fade as the animals grow.

29

The skull of an ancient crocodilian helps scientists learn how the animal has changed.

attacking enemies, such as foxes. Still, in spite of all these efforts, only a few new members of any family live to be adults.

Young and old crocodilians depend on their senses to help them avoid trouble and find food. Their hearing and sense of smell are both good. Above water, they have good sight — even in darkness. Their eyes have narrow, upright pupils that open wide at night, letting in more light than most round pupils do.

Throughout their lives, crocodilians keep growing. Young ones grow faster than old ones, especially where there is plenty of food and the weather stays warm all year. How long they survive partly depends on what kind of crocodilians they are. It is possible for American alligators to live more than seventy years, but few common caimans live past forty.

SUPERCROC!

As big as crocodiles get, they were once much bigger. In Africa's Sahara Desert, scientists uncovered a crocodile skull that is 110 million years old and as long as a tall person! They also pieced together half the animal's skeleton, which is twice the length of today's longest crocodile.

Nicknamed Supercroc, the ancient creature might have weighed 18,000 pounds (8,200 kg). It ate almost whatever its 130 teeth could grab — even dinosaurs!

Glossary

armor — a tough outer layer that protects the body.

burrows — (n) underground shelters or homes for wild animals; (v) digs holes or tunnels in the ground.

digest — to change food in the stomach and intestines so it can be used by the body.

glands — parts of the body that take materials from blood and either remove them from the body or change them into other fluids that can be used by the body.

hatchlings — animals that have newly come out of their shells.

prey — animals that are hunted by other animals for food.

pupils — the dark centers that let light into the eyes.

reptiles — a group of animals that breathe air and are covered with scales.

researcher — a person who studies something carefully in order to learn new things about it.

Index